# Study Guide

## What Great Principals Do Differently: 15 Things That Matter Most

**Beth Whitaker, Todd Whitaker, and Jeffrey Zoul**

EYE ON EDUCATION

6 DEPOT WAY WEST, SUITE 106

LARCHMONT, NY 10538

(914) 833–0551

(914) 833–0761 fax

www.eyeoneducation.com



ISBN 1-59667-035-5

10 9 8 7 6 5 4 3

Editorial and production services provided by
Richard H. Adin Freelance Editorial Services
52 Oakwood Blvd., Poughkeepsie, NY 12603-4112
(845-471-3566)

# Table of Contents

**Introduction** . . . . . . . . . . **vi**

**Section One: Chapter 1: Why Look at Great**
**Chapter 2: It's People, Not Programs** . . . . . . . . . . **1**
Understanding Key Concepts . . . . . . . . . . 1
Selecting Questions for Discussion . . . . . . . . . . 2
Eliciting Journal Responses. . . . . . . . . . 3
Interacting With Others. . . . . . . . . . 4
Taking It Back . . . . . . . . . . 5

**Section Two: Chapter 3: Who is the Variable?** . . . . . . . . . . **7**
Understanding Key Concepts . . . . . . . . . . 7
Selecting Questions for Discussion . . . . . . . . . . 8
Eliciting Journal Responses. . . . . . . . . . 9
Interacting With Others . . . . . . . . . . 10
Taking It Back. . . . . . . . . . 12

**Section Three: Chapter 4: Treat Everyone**
**with Respect, Every Day, All the Time**. . . . . . . . . . **13**
Understanding Key Concepts. . . . . . . . . . 13
Selecting Questions for Discussion. . . . . . . . . . 14
Eliciting Journal Responses . . . . . . . . . . 15
Interacting With Others . . . . . . . . . . 16
Taking It Back. . . . . . . . . . 18

**Section Four: Chapter 5: The Principal is the Filter** . . . . . . . . . . **19**
Understanding Key Concepts. . . . . . . . . . 19
Selecting Questions for Discussion. . . . . . . . . . 20
Eliciting Journal Responses . . . . . . . . . . 21
Interacting With Others . . . . . . . . . . 22
Taking It Back. . . . . . . . . . 24

**Section Five: Chapter 6: Teach the Teachers**. . . . . . . . . . **25**
Understanding Key Concepts. . . . . . . . . . 25
Selecting Questions for Discussion. . . . . . . . . . 26
Eliciting Journal Responses . . . . . . . . . . 27
Interacting With Others . . . . . . . . . . 28
Taking It Back. . . . . . . . . . 29

**Section Six: Chapter 7: Hire Great Teachers**. . . . . . . . . . **31**
Understanding Key Concepts. . . . . . . . . . 31
Selecting Questions for Discussion. . . . . . . . . . 32

Eliciting Journal Responses . . . . . . . . . . 33
Interacting With Others . . . . . . . . . . 34
Taking It Back. . . . . . . . . . 36

**Section Seven: Chapter 8: Standardized Testing**
**Chapter 9: Focus on Behavior, Then Focus on Beliefs . . . . . . . . 37**
Understanding Key Concepts. . . . . . . . . . 37
Selecting Questions for Discussion. . . . . . . . . . 38
Eliciting Journal Responses . . . . . . . . . . 39
Interacting With Others . . . . . . . . . . 40
Taking It Back. . . . . . . . . . 41

**Section Eight: Chapter 10: Loyal to Whom?**
**Chapter 11: Base Every Decision on Your Best Teachers. . . . . . 43**
Understanding Key Concepts. . . . . . . . . . 43
Selecting Questions for Discussion. . . . . . . . . . 44
Eliciting Journal Responses . . . . . . . . . . 45
Interacting With Others . . . . . . . . . . 46
Taking It Back. . . . . . . . . . 48

**Section Nine: Chapter 12: In Every Situation, Ask Who is Most Comfortable and Who is Least Comfortable . . . . . . . 49**
Understanding Key Concepts. . . . . . . . . . 49
Selecting Questions for Discussion. . . . . . . . . . 50
Eliciting Journal Responses . . . . . . . . . . 51
Interacting With Others . . . . . . . . . . 52
Taking It Back. . . . . . . . . . 54

**Section Ten: Chapter 13: Understand High Achievers. . . . . . . . . 55**
Understanding Key Concepts. . . . . . . . . . 55
Selecting Questions for Discussion. . . . . . . . . . 56
Eliciting Journal Responses . . . . . . . . . . 57
Interacting With Others . . . . . . . . . . 58
Taking It Back. . . . . . . . . . 59

**Section Eleven: Chapter 14: Make it Cool to Care . . . . . . . . . . . 61**
Understanding Key Concepts. . . . . . . . . . 61
Selecting Questions for Discussion. . . . . . . . . . 62
Eliciting Journal Responses . . . . . . . . . . 63
Interacting With Others . . . . . . . . . . 64
Taking It Back. . . . . . . . . . 67

**Section Twelve: Chapter 15: Don't Need to Repair—Always Do Repair. . . . . . . . . . 69**
Understanding Key Concepts. . . . . . . . . . 69
Selecting Questions for Discussion. . . . . . . . . . 70
Eliciting Journal Responses . . . . . . . . . . 71

Interacting With Others . . . . . . . . . . . . . . . . . . . . . . . . . . . . 72
Taking It Back. . . . . . . . . . . . . . . . . . . . . . . . . . . . . . . . . . . 74

**Section Thirteen: Chapter 16: Set Expectations at the Start of the Year; Chapter 17: Clarifying Your Core . . . . . . . . . 75**
Understanding Key Concepts. . . . . . . . . . . . . . . . . . . . . . . . . . 75
Selecting Questions for Discussion. . . . . . . . . . . . . . . . . . . . . . 76
Eliciting Journal Responses . . . . . . . . . . . . . . . . . . . . . . . . . . 77
Interacting With Others . . . . . . . . . . . . . . . . . . . . . . . . . . . . 78
Taking It Back. . . . . . . . . . . . . . . . . . . . . . . . . . . . . . . . . . . 79

**Fifteen Things That Matter Most. . . . . . . . . . . . . . . . . . . . . . 81**

# Introduction

This *Study Guide* is a tool to accompany *What Great Principals Do Differently: 15 Things That Matter Most* by Todd Whitaker. It is a practical resource for educational leaders who are examining what great principals do that sets them apart from others. This *Study Guide* assists instructors, staff developers, professors, and other educational leaders who are working with principals to hone their leadership skills. In addition, principals reading and studying Whitaker's book can use this *Study Guide* as a "workbook" for the original text. This *Study Guide* serves as a roadmap to help principals focus on the leadership beliefs, behaviors, attitudes, and commitments that positively impact teaching and learning in our classrooms and our schools.

*What Great Principals Do Differently: 15 Things That Matter Most* is filled with practical, common sense advice for principals serving at the K–12 levels. It focuses on what great principals do that sets them apart, clarifying best practices based on numerous school-based studies and visits. Whitaker's book is one that principals can read and put to use immediately. This *Study Guide* enables the facilitator to lead principals through the contents of a very important and practical book and to exhort them to not only read and understand its essential concepts, but to take what they learn back to their schools and to implement new strategies and ideas in a practical and relatively simple manner.

To stress the practicality of the book's contents, each section of this *Study Guide* is organized with the acronym ***USE IT*** in mind. The *Study Guide* is divided into several sections, each focusing on one or two chapters of Whitaker's text. The 13 sections are organized as follows:

- **Understanding Key Concepts,** which summarize the key points for each chapter in the book;
- **Selecting Questions for Discussion,** which provides a list of discussion questions that can be used in the classroom/workshop setting;
- **Eliciting Journal Responses,** is a prompt for journal writing based on the specific contents of the chapters;
- **Interacting With Others,** which offers ideas for activities to use with class/workshop participants;
- **Taking It Back,** which offers ideas for applying what is learned in the book and class/workshop in our schools.

# Section One

## Chapter 1: Why Look at Great
## Chapter 2: It's People, Not Programs

### Understanding Key Concepts

- Although principals must have a strong knowledge base in their field, what they *know* about being a school principal is subordinate in importance to what they *do* as a school principal.
- The perspective of *What Great Principals Do Differently* is threefold and based on research findings examining effective school leadership; observations at and consultations with many schools and school systems; and the personal core beliefs that guided Todd Whitaker's own work as a successful school principal.
- We can always learn from observing what great principals do. Eliminating inappropriate choices does not help as much as identifying good ideas used by successful educators.
- By studying our most effective school leaders, we learn where they focus their attention, how they spend their time and energy, and what guides their decisions.
- No matter how good our most effective principals are, they still want to be better.
- No program inherently leads to school improvement. It is the people who implement sound programs who determine the success of the school. Programs are never the solution, and they are never the problem.
- Recognizing the importance of people over programs, great principals recognize that the two primary ways to improve a school are to hire better teachers and to improve the teachers already in place.
- Great principals realize that teachers—just like students—vary widely in their individual needs and abilities. As a result, no single program will work with the same rate of success for all teachers. Programs are only solutions when they bring out the best in teachers.
- In addition to promoting whole-school growth and improvement initiatives, great principals do everything possible to promote *individual* teacher development.

## Selecting Questions for Discussion

- What do great principals see when they view their schools and the people in them?
- Why should we look at what great principals do?
- Why must we study less-effective principals and schools when determining what distinguishes those who are identified as great from those who are not great? In what ways does looking at ineffective principals and schools have limited value?
- As a school principal, what guides the decisions you make each day?
- How can you ensure that you recruit and hire the very best teachers? How can you improve the teachers already working at your school?
- Why do certain programs work so well for some teachers, but fail miserably for other teachers?

## Eliciting Journal Responses

Think of a program you implemented in recent years at your school or that was implemented at a school with which you are familiar. Which teachers adapted to the change of programs, embracing the new idea and making it work? Did any teachers resist the change? Was the program ultimately deemed a success? What determined whether or not it was successful? What should principals consider before endorsing schoolwide programs for implementation? If such programs are adopted, what can principals do to foster successful implementation while honoring individuality among teachers?

## Interacting With Others

### It's not what you do, it's how you do it...

Beginning on p. 8 of the text, Whitaker describes several "programs" that he deems neither a problem nor a solution: open classrooms, assertive discipline, whole language, direct instruction, mission statements, and standards-based assessment. Divide the class into several groups of four to six each. Ask each group to pick one of the above programs, or to pick another one that is not listed, and to discuss the relative merits of the chosen "program." Within groups, participants should discuss how the chosen program can work effectively or ineffectively, sharing any specific examples with which they are familiar from their own experience. Have each group report back whether it was the *people* involved or the *program* itself that determined the level of success.

### You don't say...

Distribute the six quotations below regarding leadership, one to each of six groups. After assigning the quotations, allow time for the groups to study and discuss the quotation. Have them discuss amongst themselves how the leadership quotation they were assigned is in some way connected to the material presented in Chapter 1 and/or Chapter 2 of the text. Ask each group to offer another quotation with which they are familiar—or even create an original one—that is connected to the material under study and to share their discussions with the group at-large.

Leadership should be more participative than directive, more enabling than performing.

A good leader inspires others with confidence in him; a great leader inspires them with confidence in themselves.

Good leaders make people feel that they're at the very heart of things, not at the periphery. Everyone feels that he or she makes a difference to the success of the organization. When that happens, people feel centered and that gives their work meaning.

Good leaders develop through a never-ending process of self-study, education, training, and experience.

A good leader is not the person who does things right, but the person who finds the right things to do.

Leaders don't force people to follow—they invite them on a journey.

## Taking It Back

Think about ways in which you want your school to improve. While you may at first focus on schoolwide improvement initiatives, recall Whitaker's research which shows that teachers value principals who not only implement whole-school growth proposals, but who are also committed to encouraging and supporting individual teacher needs for staff development. At your school, begin by asking five teachers you respect what they would most like to improve about their current practice or in what areas they would like to grow professionally. Commit to helping these teachers reach their individual self-improvement goals. Continue this in your building by making it your mission to find out what each individual teacher at your school would like to "become" during future years of their professional career. Perhaps some aspire to administrative careers. Perhaps others would like to try gifted education. Maybe others would like to move grade levels, subject areas, or into counseling. At the same time, other teachers might desire less dramatic change, wanting only to improve their classroom discipline practices or use performance assessments more effectively. As school leaders, we must recognize the needs of our individual teachers in the vital area of individual teacher development, as this will also lead to school improvement.

___

___

___

___

___

___

___

___

___

___

___

___

# Section Two

# *Chapter 3: Who is the Variable?*

## Understanding Key Concepts

- Effective principals understand that just as teachers are the variable in the classroom most responsible for student success, principals are the variables for schools and are responsible for the school's success.
- Effective principals make teachers fully aware of the impact they have in their own classrooms. As leaders, they help teachers take responsibility for their own classrooms, while accepting a higher level of responsibility for themselves.
- Research shows that effective principals view themselves as responsible for all aspects of their school, whereas less-effective principals blame outside influences for the problems in their schools and believe they have no control over outcomes.
- If everyone looks in the mirror when they ask, "Who is the variable?" we will have made tremendous strides toward school improvement.

## Selecting Questions for Discussion

- When the students of our best teachers fail, these teachers typically blame themselves. How does this concept of accepting responsibility apply to school principals?

- In what key way do effective principals differ from less-effective principals in terms of how they view their role?

- How can we as principals help our teachers take responsibility for student performance in their classrooms?

- How do effective and less-effective principals react when faced with obstacles outside of their direct control, such as budget reductions?

- Why might parents choose to send their children to a school that has just appointed an outstanding principal to lead a mediocre teaching staff over a school with a strong teaching staff but an ineffective principal?

## Eliciting Journal Responses

This chapter stresses as a key idea that what makes the difference between two schools is not a "what" at all, but, instead, a "who"; that is, teachers and principals are the true variables in schools. We have the power to make a difference in the lives of students, each other, and our schools. Consider the hypothetical scenario described on pp. 16–17 of the text regarding the two schools. How would you, as the outstanding principal with a weak faculty, begin making this the better of the two schools? Keep in mind the two-year timeline suggested in the premise and discuss how you would improve the teaching staff and the overall school.

## Interacting With Others

### Expectations—for everyone...

According to a study cited by the author, effective principals view themselves as responsible for all aspects of their school. Although all principals have high expectations for their teachers, great principals also have extremely high expectations for themselves. Working in groups of two to five, have participants reexamine the issue of expectations for principals from the perspective of students, teachers, and parents. What are a few expectations for which all stakeholders should hold all principals accountable? Have each group commit, as principals, to adhere to these expectations by drafting "We will..." statements, as in: "**We** (as principals) **will** treat all members of our school community with dignity and respect." Ask each small group to write five "We will..." statements to which they would expect themselves and other principals to adhere. Ask each group to share its list, recording answers on the board, overhead, chart paper, or computer screen. After each group has shared its list, poll the entire class about which are the five most important "We will..." statements.

### Who is responsible? Look in the mirror...

The author suggests that effective principals view themselves as responsible for all aspects of their schools. As we all know, the demands on principals are exhaustive and seem to be increasing every year. Principals are expected to fulfill numerous responsibilities including the following:

- Having vision
- Believing that the schools are for learning
- Valuing human resources
- Being a skilled communicator and listener
- Acting proactively
- Taking risks

Place each of the six headings above on a piece of chart paper. Divide participants into six groups, each beginning with one of the above areas of a principal's responsibility. Allow groups to brainstorm ways they might act on these responsibilities within their group. Post these on the walls of the room, spreading them out as much as possible. Ask each group to do a gallery stroll, spending approximately five minutes at each chart and adding to any chart additional ideas they might have for each area. Then give each individual participant six adhesive dots and direct them to place one dot on each of the six charts next to the idea they deem most useful, applicable, and important. Once all participants have placed their dots on each chart, discuss the results with the entire group.

## Notes

## Taking It Back

Upon returning to your school, take some time to compare your school to a neighboring school in terms of some measurable criterion (e.g., attendance, test scores, discipline data). Try to identify an area in which your school might be performing below the level of the comparison school. First list all the outside factors beyond your control that might (or might not) play a role in the difference between your school's performance and that of the comparison school. Next, decide on what you *can* control that might improve your own school's performance. Share your thoughts with other leaders at your school and devise a plan committed to improving your school in this targeted area.

# Section Three

# *Chapter 4: Treat Everyone with Respect, Every Day, All the Time*

## Understanding Key Concepts

- One hallmark of an effective principal is how the principal treats people—with dignity and respect each and every day.
- If we, as principals, treat a student or staff member rudely, that person will never forget it, nor will anyone who witnessed it.
- Teachers know the difference between right and wrong and want their principals to deal with their irresponsible peers—but in an appropriate and professional manner.
- Our behaviors as principals are much more obvious to all with whom we come in contact than our beliefs. The principal who sets a positive tone can influence the interactions of everyone in the school.
- A key responsibility of an effective leader is to create a positive atmosphere.
- Praise can be a powerful motivator and reinforcer, if used properly. Used correctly, it is impossible to praise too much.
- Principals who consistently model their expectations regarding how people should be treated encourage all those within the school community to do the same.

## Selecting Questions for Discussion

- What must principals do to keep the best teachers on their side when dealing with ineffective teachers?

- Why is it so important for principals to treat all teachers in a dignified and respectful manner each and every day?

- What is the one central concept Whitaker identifies as key to using praise effectively? Why is this so important?

- Identify some of the reasons principals give for not praising teachers. What are possible responses to these reasons?

- Whitaker suggests that how often we praise others is a choice and that whenever we choose to praise another person, at least two people feel better. Who are these two people? Discuss how the entire school can subsequently benefit as a result of this simple act.

## Eliciting Journal Responses

Write about a time when you lost your temper or patience with a student or teacher at your school. How did you react and how did this make you feel? Did your relationship with this student or teacher change as a result? Whitaker suggests that our real challenge is to treat *everyone* at our school with dignity and respect *every* day. Although seemingly simple, as principals we face a multitude of growing demands and constraints. Why is it still so important to focus on the simple concept of treating our students and teachers with dignity and respect?

## Interacting With Others

### Our cup runneth over!

Whitaker emphasizes that focusing on the positive elements of our schools will give us more drive and energy as we face our daily work. Divide into groups of three to five. Provide each group with a piece of chart paper with a large cup or glass drawn on it and a package of sticky notes. Instruct the groups that they are to "fill" their cup with examples of great things happening in their schools. Write brief thoughts and descriptions on the sticky notes and place them inside the cup. Continue working until each cup is filled with positive, productive things happening in their schools. Allow time for individuals to share within their groups. Then have each group choose and present its "Top Five" positive ideas with the entire group. Post these charts for all to read and discuss.

### Raise the praise—effectively...

Whitaker reminds us of the power of praise. When praising, make sure to use nonjudgmental language. The key is to express your own feelings in the form of an "I" statement, instead of making a judgment about the other person or her/his work with a "You" statement. For example:

Try: "I respect the way you lead your team" rather than: "You are a good teacher."

Try: "I was impressed with the way you ran the meeting" rather than: "You ran the meeting well."

When praising, remember to be specific, clean, sincere, and immediate. Ask each participant to read the following statements regarding recognizing effective praise according to the guidelines above. After individuals have completed the ten exercises, have them share their answers with a classmate.

## Recognizing Effective Praise

*Instructions:* Place an "E" by examples of effective praise and an "I" by examples of ineffective praise. Change ineffective praise to effective praise. Discuss with group members your thoughts about each statement. Share ways that any ineffective statements can be improved.

____ 1. I'm glad you remembered to bring your class lists to the meeting. That was good thinking.

____ 2. I appreciate that you remembered to bring your emergency folder. I hope you won't forget next time.

____ 3. For a first-year teacher, you did very well.

____ 4. The room looks really nice. Your bulletin board is meaningful to your unit.

____ 5. Well, now, you look much more professional without the baggie sweat pants.

____ 6. I hear you're helping Mr. Smith with his science lessons. That's nice. I am sure he appreciates your encouragement.

____ 7. It was so nice when you ran the awards assembly last year. Could you do that again?

____ 8. (To the teacher who has just presented at a faculty meeting.) Good job!

____ 9. Learning new technology is difficult. I'm glad you are trying.

____ 10. Mrs. Jones, your students were much better behaved today than at the last assembly.

## Notes

## Taking It Back

On pp. 24–25, Whitaker notes several reasons principals and teachers give for not praising those with whom they work. Make the time during the next five school days to praise at least five different students and five different teachers. For the students, this should be in the form of a phone call to parents praising a specific behavior or accomplishment, or a postcard or handwritten note sent home in the mail. For teachers, this might be done in the form of a positive note placed in teacher mailboxes, a card sent to the teacher through the mail, or even a nice note to the teacher's parents, letting them know how much your school values their child. Report back at the next session as to whether the time invested was worth it based on the reactions you received.

# Section Four

# *Chapter 5: The Principal is the Filter*

## Understanding Key Concepts

- Effective principals realize that they are the filters for the day-to-day reality of the school and that their behavior sets the tone for all.
- Principals must serve as a filter for which information is shared with teachers and other stakeholders. By sparing others unnecessary bad news, the principal creates a more productive environment.
- The principal is the most significant influence on the entire school; the principal's focus becomes the school's focus. We must keep our attention on issues that matter, rather than diverting effort and energy to trivial annoyances.
- Principals use regular faculty meetings as staff development opportunities.
- Regardless of the purpose, content, or focus of a faculty meeting, the principal's additional challenge should be to have teachers leave the meeting more excited about teaching tomorrow than they were about teaching today.
- Great principals understand that perceptions can become reality. One of the best ways to alter negative perceptions is to provide other perceptions.
- Consciously, or not, principals *decide* the tone of the school.

## Selecting Questions for Discussion

- Explain how our responses as principals to questions and situations can affect teachers within the school.
- How should principals determine which information they should filter out and not share with staff members?
- What is the result when a principal shares with a teacher an unpleasant situation that the principal had with an angry parent?
- What is a determining factor in whether the teachers within our schools work with us or against us?
- How can principals work to change the perceptions of those teachers who complain about their students and other problems at their schools?

## Eliciting Journal Responses

Whitaker offers several examples of situations in which leaders should have "filtered out" a minor annoyance. Consider the examples offered, including "thumping," the angry parent, and the "potentially bad legislation." Discuss in writing other types of negative incidents you face each day that can be filtered out and not passed along to teachers. At times, of course, we must share negative information of significance with our teachers. What is the most effective way to share such news? How can we openly discuss such news with our teachers without shifting their energy to unproductive worrying?

## Interacting With Others

### Circle of friends...

Arrange the group into two circles—an "inner" circle and an "outer" circle—one inside the other, with the participants in the inner circle facing the people in the outer circle. Have the person in the inner circle relate an example of negativity at their school. The person in the outer circle should listen carefully and offer suggestions for dealing with this negativity. After approximately five minutes, have the inner circle rotate three places to the right. Repeat the activity, but this time have the person in the outer circle share a negative scenario. Repeat one or two additional times. Then, as a large group, share what was learned. Did most participants share similar stories? What examples of negativity are principals faced with regularly? What were the most useful strategies for dealing with negativity?

### Setting the tone...

Principals, consciously or not, decide the tone of the school. Here are ten suggestions principals can use to set the tone. Have participants review the ten ideas with a partner or small group and then list at least two or three tangible ways to implement each suggestion.

1. **Support new teachers**

   Nearly one-third of new U.S. teachers leave the profession during their first three years. Almost half leave during their first five years. The price of high turnover is enormous in terms of money, productivity, and morale.

2. **Clue into climate**

   What happens at faculty meetings? What traditions and ceremonies do teachers and staff have to celebrate successes? These are elements of school climate, the underlying attitudes and expectations of your employees. Climate affects morale enormously.

3. **Empower teachers and staff**

   People are happiest when they have some control over their work environment. Autocratic, top-down leadership tends to quash teacher and employee morale.

4. **Recognize and reward teachers and staff**

   Letting teachers know they're doing a good job and recognizing their achievements publicly goes a long way toward making them feel appreciated.

5. **Don't ignore administrator morale**

   Unhappy administrators hurt morale.

6. **Deal with student discipline**

   Disruptive student behavior damages teacher morale and causes some teachers to leave. New teachers, in particular, have trouble with classroom management, and teachers who leave say they don't feel adequately backed up by principals when it comes to disciplining individual students.

7. **Treat teachers like professionals**

   Teachers need professional development and time to collaborate with colleagues. If they know that, like their students, they are expected to be continuous learners, they see themselves as professionals.

8. **Ask employees what's going on**

   Gathering employee input, whether through informal chat sessions or by a written school survey, gives the staff a chance to be heard on important issues. It also can alert administrators and others to potential problems.

9. **Keep facilities tidy**

   Teachers who work every day in crumbling, dirty, and neglected buildings are bound to feel that their work isn't especially valued.

10. **Develop emotional understanding**

    Everyone needs to feel emotional support from the person they work for. Being empathetic and appreciating a well-done job are just two ways we can provide emotional support to our employees. Good leaders do this to help teachers work at their highest levels.

## Notes

## Taking It Back

Upon returning to your school, make a conscious decision to filter out negative situations that you face, whether they come from outside or within the school. Respond cheerfully to any staff member who asks how you are doing. Politely redirect any negative comments made by a staff member. Brag about your students and teachers each day to anyone who will listen. Tell students at the end of each day that you can't wait to return to school the following day because you are so excited about what they will be learning. After doing this for several consecutive days, record in your study guides any changes you noticed in your own perspective or that of others, including students and teachers at your school.

# Section Five

# *Chapter 6: Teach the Teachers*

## Understanding Key Concepts

- Outstanding principals know that their primary role is to teach the teachers. Great principals focus on students by focusing on teachers.
- If we want our teachers to do better, we must teach them how. We cannot expect a person to do better if they do not know a better way.
- Our students benefit from observing teachers working together successfully. Great principals find ways for teachers to collaborate in order to improve school and student performance.
- Great principals do not let the many demands on their time prevent them from improving teacher effectiveness.
- Effective principals take time to get into the classrooms of troubled teachers and help build their skills.
- The more time that principals spend building the skills of their teachers, the less they are drained by reacting to the results of ineffective teaching practices.
- One of the principal's most important jobs is getting into classrooms. When teachers see us in their classrooms, they see how we expect them to interact with students.
- Great principals do not let teachers who drag their feet keep others from making a difference.
- Collaboration among classroom teachers is one of the most basic and effective ways to improve instruction. Because our goal is to help all teachers to become as good as our best teachers, a good place to start is by giving everyone a chance to observe each other. When we use our best teachers as positive role models, we multiply their productivity and help other teachers improve their own performance.

## Selecting Questions for Discussion

- Students are the most important people in the school. How can principals best help their students?

- If it is true, as Whitaker surmises, that all teachers do the best they can in terms of classroom management, what must we do as principals to help them improve if they are struggling in this critical area?

- Most principals realize that the majority of discipline referrals they receive emanate from the classrooms of only a few teachers. What should principals do to address this proactively rather than reactively?

- Why is it important for teachers to get out of their own classrooms and observe one another teaching?

- According to Whitaker, what is a potential obstacle a principal faces in getting teachers to observe each other? How do great principals deal with this obstacle?

## Eliciting Journal Responses

Describe three of the best teachers at your school. What makes them stand out? What is it about them that you wish all teachers at your school had? Think about three other teachers who might benefit from observing these three superstars in action. Would they be able to improve their own performance after observing their colleague? Would the superstar teacher learn something through this process as well? Approached carefully, would both the superstar and mediocre teacher be willing to observe in each other's classrooms? In what ways could this benefit your students and improve your school?

## Interacting With Others

### You oughta be in pictures...

The facilitator could make a CD with clips from several movies to enhance this activity, but it is probably not necessary as most educators have seen several of these movies. Either way, discuss these and other movies participants have seen that focus on an educator as a central character. Make a list of common characteristics each teacher in the various movies possesses. Generate a whole-group list. Have participants share with a classmate how the teacher-character in one of the films reminds them of a teacher at their own school or a teacher who they had at one point in time. Here is a list of some films in which the teacher is a central character:

- Mr. Holland's Opus
- Goodbye Mr. Chips
- October Sky
- Stand and Deliver
- Dangerous Minds
- To Sir with Love
- The Blackboard Jungle
- Up the Down Staircase
- Teacher
- Dead Poets Society

### Featuring our own teachers...

Have participants work with a group of principals from similar schools (e.g., elementary, middle, high) to develop a plan that can be implemented at their schools whereby teachers are given opportunities to observe other teachers. Ask participants to consider how they will get the least-effective teachers into the most-effective teachers' classrooms without hurt feelings. Also, have them discuss if funds will be needed, what kind of preparation and follow up teachers would be required to do, whether to encourage or require some sort of feedback or share session after the observation, and other questions that might arise. Have each group share its thoughts with the large group.

## Taking It Back

For the next five school days, make it a point to get into classrooms throughout the school building as much as possible. You might even try gathering some paperwork you need to complete and bring it into several classrooms to work on throughout the day. While you are visiting and working in classrooms, take note of what students are learning. As you walk around classrooms while students are working independently, ask them quietly, "What are you learning?" Make mental records of student responses. Share five of the more interesting responses you hear with your staff via an e-mail. If you notice something in a classroom that seems to be interfering with student learning, make a commitment to ask the teacher for his/her own thoughts regarding your observation, and offer ideas for improvement.

# Section Six

# *Chapter 7: Hire Great Teachers*

## Understanding Key Concepts

- A principal's single most precious commodity is an opening on the teaching staff. The quickest way to improve your school is to hire great teachers at every opportunity. Great principals hire teachers who are better than those teachers they are replacing.
- In hiring new teachers, great principals want the school to become more like the new teacher instead of the other way around. Hiring teachers who will "fit right in" should not be the primary goal of the principal.
- Great principals hire dynamic teachers and strive to keep them that way. They look for teachers who will not only be great in the classroom, but who will also be influential in the school.
- Many of the qualities great principals look for—love of students, positive attitude, congenial personality—are more inherent than learned. Consequently, great principals value such overall talent over specific technique.
- If we hire highly talented teachers, they will thrive wherever we put them and will help make our school better.
- There must be no pecking order in our schools. Great principals make decisions about teachers based on each individual's effectiveness and contributions rather than on seniority.
- New teacher induction should start during the interviewing process through skillful and strategic questioning and establishing expectations.

## Selecting Questions for Discussion

- Why is hiring great teachers so monumentally important to great principals?
- Why does Whitaker downplay the importance of hiring teachers who are "a good match"?
- What is the essential variable in hiring new teachers? What are some factors that are secondary in importance to this core indicator of future success?
- How can principals begin to send the message that there is no pecking order and that effectiveness is valued over seniority?
- Discuss several ways you can informally begin the process of induction during the interview.
- How can principals discreetly let new teachers know which colleagues they should choose as role models?

## Eliciting Journal Responses

Whitaker states that he would rather hire a new teacher with "a jarful of talent and a thimbleful of technique than the other way around." Reflect on this statement and what it means to you. Do you agree or disagree? What constitutes "talent" when looking for great teachers? What constitutes "technique"? How heavily should you value factors such as advanced degrees and years of experience?

## Interacting With Others

### Top teaching traits...

Have each individual participant brainstorm a list of approximately ten traits they look for when hiring new teachers. Next, have them share their lists with a partner. After they have had a chance to share their thoughts on characteristics they value in new teacher candidates, regroup participants into small groups of three or four. Distribute the following list of teacher traits, and ask each group to prioritize these traits from 1–15, with number 1 being the most essential characteristic necessary. Have each group report back to the large group and compare rankings. Discuss any glaring difference—or similarities—among the various group rankings.

_____ Flexibility

_____ Organization

_____ Ability to build success into the class

_____ Ability to communicate clearly

_____ Ability to create a pleasant atmosphere

_____ Ability to differentiate instruction

_____ Ability to establish successful classroom management

_____ Enthusiasm

_____ High expectations

_____ Content knowledge

_____ Good people skills (with students, staff, parents)

_____ Ability to pace instruction.

_____ Ability to ask effective questions.

_____ Good attitude

_____ Ability to teach actively

### Induction starts at the interview...

Whitaker suggests that we need to begin the induction process as early as during the interview (once we have determined that the teaching candidate is a strong prospect). Below is another list of traits that many principals find desirable when seeking out new teachers. How can we (a) ask probing questions that ensure we are learning whether the candidate possesses these characteristics and (b) begin the induction process by setting expectations regarding each of these traits? Have the group work in pairs. Distribute the following list to each pair of participants. Ask each principal to take turns role playing the interview scenario, focusing on one key trait at a time. The "interviewing" principal should attempt to ask realistic questions aimed at discerning whether the "candidate" possesses the identified trait. The "interviewee" principal should answer the questions in a way that he/she believes is most likely a favorable reply. The "interviewing" principals should practice "inducting" the candidate by letting the candidate know their expectations regarding the trait and how this might come up in their role as a teacher at their schools. In pairs, take turns role playing the principal and the teacher candidate, moving through the list of key teacher traits below:

- Teachers must…
  - Be flexible
  - Create a pleasant atmosphere
  - Hold high expectations
  - Build success into their class
  - Differentiate instruction
  - Question effectively
  - Communicate clearly
  - Maintain good people skills
  - Establish successful classroom management
  - Exhibit enthusiasm
  - Know their content
  - Be organized
  - Teach actively
  - Maintain a good attitude

## Notes

## Taking It Back

Upon returning to your school, jot down the names of five "superstar" teachers at your school. Try to pick teachers at various grade levels and/or subject areas. For each teacher, list five or six characteristics that make them stand out in your mind as outstanding teachers and members of your school community. From these five lists, choose the traits you listed most often.

Before beginning the next part of this activity, be very aware of the school dynamic in which you work. It is recommended to keep this focused on the teaching traits and characteristics and not use specific teacher names in this activity. You are focusing on improving your entire staff. Overtly making some teachers look better than the rest can sometimes cause unnecessary ill will. You can always privately let these teachers know how much you value their expertise and performance.

Continue this activity by writing a paragraph (without identifying the teachers' names) about each trait you value most and share this with your staff in a memo or e-mail, perhaps citing examples you notice each day as you visit classrooms throughout your school. In addition to listing general traits of these educators, pinpoint two or three specific practices these master teachers exhibit in their classrooms that you would like all members of your faculty to learn.

# Section Seven

# *Chapter 8: Standardized Testing*
# *Chapter 9: Focus on Behavior, Then Focus on Beliefs*

## Understanding Key Concepts

- Core issues, such as teacher morale, school culture and climate, and student behavior, have been central to our schools for decades and will remain essential for decades to come.
- Great principals focus on enduring core values and spend less time and energy on the hot-button issues that would shift their attention from what really matters.
- Regardless of what we believe about standardized testing, as principals we must deal with the reality of testing and behave accordingly. We must shift our focus away from beliefs and center on behaviors.
- Effective principals do not let standardized tests consume the entire school, yet realize that success on standardized tests allows for greater autonomy to do what they believe is best for students.
- Effective principals describe student achievement in much broader terms than less-effective principals, listing not only test scores, but also student social skills, behavior, responsibility, involvement in school, and similar characteristics as important components of student success.
- The greatest impediment to change is fear, especially fear of the unknown. Even if a new approach is guaranteed to work, the transition is scary. Great principals convince teachers to change not by persuading them to change their beliefs, but by getting them to change their behaviors.
- When we teach our faculty strategies for effecting change, we empower them and can reasonably expect them to change their behavior. Effective principals do not waste time or energy trying to persuade everyone that a new way will be better than the old way. They realize that changing behaviors paves the way for changing beliefs.

## Selecting Questions for Discussion

- What are two key questions we should ask in determining the role of standardized tests? What is the relationship between these two questions?

- How do great principals manage to get all teachers on the same page regarding standardized testing despite the fact that opinions vary so widely?

- In the matter of standardized testing—and any other potentially controversial topic—how do the most effective leaders decide to deal with the issue when talking with teachers and other stakeholders?

- Effective principals realize the risk of making standardized tests and testing standards the center of the school's business. Explain this risk and what, instead, should guide our decision making.

- Why is it more effective and productive for principals to focus on teacher behaviors than on teacher beliefs?

- Explain Whitaker's suggestions in the section "Let's Call Those Parents," in Chapter 9, for getting teachers to initiate regular contacts with parents.

- Instead of wasting time and energy trying to persuade reluctant teachers to "buy in" to a new system or idea, how do effective principals ensure that teachers become interested and begin to change?

## Eliciting Journal Responses

In Chapter 9, Whitaker stresses that although great principals respect the beliefs of all teachers, it is often more helpful to focus on behaviors, rather than beliefs, when attempting to implement change. He offers a few examples of change initiatives principals might want to make in terms of teacher behavior, including getting teachers to call parents regularly or use praise more frequently. Think of one area at your own school in which you would like to see the vast majority of your teachers change or grow. Describe how getting your teachers to change would improve your school. What can you do to change teacher behaviors so that this change can be effected?

## Interacting With Others

### Two key questions...

The author maintains that it is time to move away from debating the merits of standardized testing and focus instead on our behaviors related to the issue of testing. In groups of five or fewer, have participants discuss the two key questions he poses: (a) What should our schools be doing? (b) What do standardized tests measure? Have each group portray their answers pictorially, using a framework similar to that offered in Figures 1 and 2 on p. 53 of the text. Have each group describe those things that standardized tests fail to measure, but which are vitally important to any school by creating a Top Ten list of the most important things schools must do that are not measured by standardized testing. At the same time, have each group create another Top Ten list offering the most important reasons for schools to demonstrate success on standardized tests. Have groups draw their circles and write their Top Ten lists on chart paper. Ask each group to present its findings.

### Actions speak louder than words...

Arrange participants into groups of three or four. Have them develop and share a skit that illustrates how a teacher, administrator, or student demonstrates through their behavior a positive or negative image or attitude. Look to the example of the teacher who put her hands on her hips and sighed when she was displeased. Remind them to concentrate on and discuss the effects of their body language. Many people do not realize that their actions are speaking much louder that their words!

### Notes

## Taking It Back

Upon returning to your school, list five belief statements regarding education that you predict nearly all your teachers would endorse. You might consider some or all of the following: (a) All kids can learn; (b) The work we do at our school is important; (c) We will not give up on students; (d) Communicating with parents is important; and (e) Teacher and student attendance impacts student learning. Try to take these and/or other belief statements and change them into value statements or commitments that show what behaviors you and your staff are willing to exhibit to make these beliefs a living reality within your school community. Enlist the support of other leaders at your school in identifying one or two key behaviors you believe the majority of your staff is willing to support, and ask for everyone to change their behavior to reflect this point of emphasis.

# Section Eight

## Chapter 10: Loyal to Whom?
## Chapter 11: Base Every Decision on Your Best Teachers

### Understanding Key Concepts

- All principals would like their teachers to be loyal to them. Effective principals expect their teachers to be loyal to the students. Great principals are loyal to their students, to their teachers, and to their school.
- Loyalty means making decisions based on what is best for *all* students. We cannot make a decision based on what is best for *one* student at the expense of the other students.
- Effective principals expect teachers to place the needs of their students ahead of their own personal desires, and they expect no less from themselves. Otherwise, we shift our focus from the students to ourselves.
- Talented teachers are often strong willed people who may challenge our decisions and even strongly oppose them. However, if their focus is consistently on the students, perhaps they are right.
- If we want our schools to be better, we will find ways to focus on our best teachers. The best principals base every decision on their best teachers.
- A teacher can be classified as Superstar, Backbone, or Mediocre. A superstar is a teacher who is remembered by his/her former students, who is regularly requested by parents, and who is respected by his/her peers. If this teacher left your school, you would probably not be able to hire another teacher as good to replace him/her.
- The most effective principals understand that their school will go as far as their best teachers take it; consequently, they value their superstar teachers.
- Effective principals consult their best teachers before attempting to implement change. They have the confidence to seek input in advance of change initiatives and feedback after the fact.
- Effective principals understand that the hardest teacher to move forward is the first one, not the last one. Once the superstars move forward, the backbones will move with them.
- Our superstars will always be effective, but if we do not value their input, they will limit their influence to their individual classrooms. We need our superstars to influence the entire school.
- Effective principals do not issue orders and directives to the entire staff. Instead, they only address those teachers who are creating the problem.

## Selecting Questions for Discussion

- Why is it more important for our teachers to be loyal to our students than to ourselves?
- In dealing with staff members, what focus should guide us to make the right decision?
- How can two people both be right even when they vehemently disagree?
- Why must principals base their decisions on the very best teachers in the school?
- Typically, what percentage of a faculty is comprised of "superstar" teachers?
- If our very best teachers do not think something is a good idea, should we still proceed with the idea? Why or why not?
- Why do we ask all teachers for input? Why do we ask our superstar teachers for input?
- Why must we use discretion when asking our superstar teachers for input?

## Eliciting Journal Responses

In these chapters, Whitaker discusses being loyal to students and basing our own decisions on our very best people. Think about your very best teachers. Are they loyal to their students? How does this impact your own job as principal? Discuss in writing one or two teachers with whom you consult informally when you are considering whether to implement change or make a significant decision related to the school. Do these teachers tend to offer keen insights? Are they forthright, even if their answers may not be the ones you were hoping for? How do you react to such feedback? Would you still move forward with an idea for change if one or two of your best teachers were opposed?

## Interacting With Others

### Decisions, decisions, decisions…

Divide principals into groups based on whether they serve at the elementary, middle, or high school level, making sure that you have no more than four or five participants in each group. Have each level respond to their respective scenario.

- *Elementary:* A teacher has proposed that all students remain silent during the first ten minutes of lunch each day.
- *Middle:* A teacher has proposed that the school adopt a "silent transition" policy, whereby students must be silent in the corridors during class changes.
- *High:* A teacher has proposed that the school adopt a "no zero" policy, whereby teachers cannot assign the grade of 0 for any assignment, but must assign an "Incomplete" instead until the student makes up the work.

Within their grade-alike groups, have participants discuss each proposal, considering three important questions in coming to a decision: (a) What is the purpose of the proposal? (b) Will the proposal accomplish this purpose? (c) What will the best teachers at my school think about this change? Share thoughts within groups and report back to the large group, letting everyone know which decision you arrived at and whether there was unanimity among group members.

### Spelling it out…

Arrange principals in small groups. Have each group create a definition of loyalty. Share and discuss definitions with large group. Next, post the following components of loyalty and have the large group compare their definitions with these descriptors.

Loyalty

Loyalty is:

- Being there to help someone whenever they need it
- Supporting students and teachers and not laughing at them when they need help
- Keeping a promise

- Considering what is best for students despite what you or your teachers may want or need
- Helping others when they need you
- Helping someone with a problem as if it were your own
- Honoring a commitment
- Being true to yourself and others
- Looking out for the best interests of everyone involved

Reorganize principals into new small groups and ask them to come up with a word or phrase associated with loyalty that begins with or incorporates each letter of the word "Loyalty" itself. Present the results on chart paper.

**L**

**O**

**Y**

**A**

**L**

**T**

**Y**

## Notes

## Taking It Back

At every school, principals must decide how to deal with staff members who act inappropriately. For example, Whitaker offers an example of teachers who abuse the copy machine, making inordinate amounts of copies on a regular basis. Principals face a number of similar such trivial issues in which just a few teachers create a problem for the entire school. Think of such a situation at your own school. Knowing that issuing edicts to the entire staff to address the indiscretions of a few is counterproductive, what do you/will you do? Call a principal at another school with whom you enjoy a collegial relationship and ask how he/she handles such situations. Are there times when you have issued schoolwide directives? Share your thoughts and insights gained at the next session.

# Section Nine

# *Chapter 12: In Every Situation, Ask Who is Most Comfortable and Who is Least Comfortable*

## Understanding Key Concepts

- All principals face the challenge of balancing rules and guidelines with those times when we need to make exceptions to the established rules.
- All principals must establish internal ground rules for making decisions in such instances. One internal standard that supports effective leadership is to always ask, when making decisions, "Who is most comfortable and who is least comfortable in this situation?"
- As principals, we want those who are uncomfortable to change in a positive direction; we do not want to create an uncomfortable situation for our best teachers.
- Positive staff members will align themselves on the side of the principal when we deal effectively with less-positive staff.
- Great principals avoid sending general directives or reminders to all students, teachers, or parents. Instead, they try to approach only those students, teachers, or parents who are responsible for the problem.
- When principals must send out a communication to an entire group, they should focus on the positive people and treat everyone as if they were good. Such notes reinforce good behavior and make those exhibiting noncompliance uncomfortable.
- Teachers should not punish an entire class for the misbehavior of a few students. Principals, too, should follow this guideline.
- Applied consistently, the question, "Who is most comfortable and who is least comfortable?" can bring clarity to our decision making.

## Selecting Questions for Discussion

- Why must principals—at times—make decisions that are exceptions to explicit rules and guidelines? When does this situation most often arise?

- Why does the landlord described in the book put effort into remodeling apartments of tenants he deems undesirable? How does this apply to the way we might deal with mediocre teachers?

- What happens when teachers punish the entire class for the misbehavior of a few? How do the misbehaving kids feel? How do the behaving students feel?

- What are the repercussions of arguing with a parent?

- Reflect on the "pay-for-performance" scenario Whitaker describes. Why does he suggest that the perspectives of the entire faculty were not the decisive factor regarding the program's merit?

## Eliciting Journal Responses

The author proposes that we treat everyone as if they were good because it will make those who are good feel affirmed and it will make all others feel uncomfortable. Consider the graffiti in bathroom stalls the author references. What did this particular school do in an effort to eliminate graffiti? Would such a decision likely accomplish the purpose? How will the best students feel about this decision? How about the perpetrators? Consider an alternate way of dealing with this student issue in which you treat every student as if they were good.

## Interacting With Others

### Dear parents...

On pp. 75–76 of the text, Whitaker shares a memo he saw sent home to all parents regarding picking up their children on time. He also includes an alternative letter that is just as effective as a reminder to the parents who are the problem, while reinforcing the good behavior of the majority of the parents. In groups of three to five, brainstorm other issues that arise each year that result in a letter home to parents (e.g., attendance, signing and returning paperwork, tardiness, making up work, discipline, sending children with appropriate materials). Ask each group to choose one topic and write two versions of a letter to parents addressing the issue. The first letter should be written in the "traditional" approach, targeting all parents equally. The second letter should be written in the alternative style, attempting to make the parents who act correctly feel comfortable, while perhaps making the others feel slightly uncomfortable in the hopes they will change the behavior.

### Freeze frame...

Have participants work in pairs and begin role-playing one of the situations listed below in front of the class. In each situation, have principals concentrate on how to correct the undesirable behavior by remembering who is most comfortable and who is least comfortable. The role-players improvise the scene, but at any moment anyone in the class (including the facilitator) can say "FREEZE." The role-players must stop where they are. Then the person who froze the action gets up, taps one of the role-players on the shoulder, and takes his or her place in the scene. The new role-player now resumes the scene by talking first, but can introduce any new dialogue or action he or she wishes. The new role-player can modify the scene slightly, take it in a very different direction, or completely change the topic of the scene. The role-players continue to improvise the new scene until someone else from the class says "FREEZE" and steps in to alter the scene once again. This process of improvising, freezing, and altering the scene continues until as many people as desired have taken turns participating in the role play. Here are the situations:

- A small number of parents are dropping off fast-food lunches in the front office to be delivered to children during their lunch time. Children are not allowed to eat these lunches in the cafeteria.
- Teachers forgetting to take attendance, causing the attendance list to be delayed each day.

- Anything to do with a dress code (teachers or students).
- Students using inappropriate websites for research.
- Parents "helping" children too much with school projects.

## Notes

## Taking It Back

Upon returning to your school, examine any student handbooks, parent communications, course outlines, syllabi, and codes of conducts you can locate. Examine each of the available documents and apply the *Who is most comfortable and who is least comfortable in this situation?* standard. Find any examples of language that might make your best stakeholders feel uncomfortable while doing little to address those who might truly need to understand the directives and change their behavior. Bring back any examples you can find to share at the next class session.

# Section Ten

# *Chapter 13: Understand High Achievers*

## Understanding Key Concepts

- One of a principal's greatest challenges is working successfully with high-achieving teachers. They do so much for our schools that we must understand these key people, remain sensitive to their needs, and maximize their ability.
- The very best leaders ignore minor errors. High achievers emotionally deflate when they have their shortcomings pointed out by someone else.
- If a principal harps on minor errors, the faculty shies away from and avoids interaction with that principal.
- Truly outstanding teachers need two things from principals to make them content and motivated: autonomy and recognition.
- Great principals allow high-achieving teachers to take risks. They do not attempt to control the behavior of less positive faculty members by establishing rules. Every time we put a rule in place, good people follow it and thus lose autonomy. Those for whom it was intended will ignore it anyway.
- Effective leaders consistently acknowledge that what their best teachers do is special and different. Great principals make certain that these superstar teachers know that they are valued and that they make a difference in the lives of students.
- Principals must delegate anything that anyone else can do because there are simply too many things that *only* the principal can do.
- The same rule applies for high-achieving teachers. Do not ask them to do something that another teacher can do. If we assign our best teachers unimportant tasks, we waste a valuable resource. If we plan ahead and ask others to take on less-essential tasks, we protect our high achievers and gain the involvement of other staff members.
- High achievers are among the first to leave a school if they do not feel valued and important. If we do not take care of them, someone else will, and we will have squandered our most valuable resource.

## Selecting Questions for Discussion

- Why is it sometimes challenging for principals to work successfully with our highest-achieving teachers?

- Discuss criticism and praise, specifically as they relate to high-achieving teachers. How do our superstar teachers react to criticism? To praise?

- Why is it important to allow our best teachers to take risks, even when we are not sure they will succeed?

- Discuss Whitaker's rule of thumb for principals in terms of delegating responsibility. Do you agree? Why or why not? How does this rule also apply to our high-achieving teachers?

- If a high-achieving teacher and a griping teacher are both unhappy, which is more likely to leave a school? Why? How can we keep our best teachers in place? How can we encourage our less-than-stellar teachers to look elsewhere?

## Eliciting Journal Responses

Whitaker stresses that principals must overlook what he calls "minor errors." Principals vary widely on what they might consider a "minor" error. Some are passionate about professional attire and timeliness, whereas others may consider these minor areas of focus. What are some errors you are willing to overlook, particularly as they relate to your high-achieving teachers? How would student success be impacted if you completely overlooked these errors? On the other hand, what are a few "nonnegotiables" for you as principal; that is, "errors" that you feel you cannot overlook? If you are a veteran principal, have your views on this changed over time? If you are a new principal, what are you willing to overlook in this area?

## Interacting With Others

### Evaluating—and valuing—high achievers...

On p. 85 of the book, Whitaker discusses the challenges of teacher evaluations, in particular evaluating our high-achieving teachers, whose value to the school cannot always be captured in a standard teacher evaluation form. Organize participants into five groups. Have them discuss successes and frustrations they have experienced with various teacher evaluation processes. Distribute one of the following five statements to each of the five groups. Have them examine the assigned statement relating to teacher evaluation in light of high achieving teachers:

- Place the teacher at the center of evaluation activity.
- Use more than one person to judge teacher quality and performance.
- Use multiple data sources to inform judgments about teachers.
- Spend extensive time and other resources needed to recognize good teaching.
- Use the results of teacher evaluation to encourage personal professional dossier building.

After each group receives one of the above statements, ask them to brainstorm ways of incorporating the statement into their own teacher evaluation practices, particularly for their high achievers. How can each of the above be implemented in a way that enhances the professional growth of our superstar teachers? Ask each group to share with the large group the statement they analyzed and ideas they came up with.

### Getting the right teachers...

Ask individual participants to take several minutes to list the desired qualities of a high-achieving teacher. Next, have them share these lists with a classmate and combine the lists into one streamlined list. Share and discuss with a group of four to five participants and create one new, revised group list. Share and discuss with the whole group and create one final list of revised qualities. Take this list and work with a new group of three to four participants and create questions and scenarios to use in an interview setting to determine if a teaching candidate possesses the desired qualities of a high-achieving teacher.

## Taking It Back

Consider the issue of delegating responsibilities, both for yourself as principal and your high-achieving staff. List your name and the names of any assistant principals and five high-achieving teachers. Try to find at least one duty and/or responsibility assigned to each of these names that, upon reflection, seems less than significant to the core work of your school, which could be delegated to another staff member. List the names of staff members who could assume these responsibilities. Keep in mind that you want your highest achieving staff members to focus on those things that only they can do. By delegating less-significant responsibilities, you free them up for more important work and include other staff members at the same time. Keep in mind that these activities should not be routine things that everyone takes a turn doing (e.g., bus duty, recess duty).

# Section Eleven

## *Chapter 14: Make it Cool to Care*

### Understanding Key Concepts

- Effective principals have a strong core of beliefs that guide their decisions and define their vision for their schools.
- The clearer we are about our own beliefs, the more effective we can be in working toward them.
- Our core beliefs can be extremely simple, yet they frame the way we work in schools.
- Getting people at your school to do the current thing is fine; getting them to do the right thing is essential.
- Treating people with dignity and respect; having a positive attitude; teaching teachers how to treat students; understanding that it is people, not programs, that make a difference; hiring great teachers; and making decisions based on your best people are all ways to cultivate a school environment in which it is cool to care.
- Every principal needs to know which teachers are the legends within the school and must work to make sure the teachers on the pedestal are the best teachers.
- Great principals do the right thing no matter what else is happening.
- Once we have presented logical reasons for change clearly, resistant teachers will not be swayed by further argument. We must understand that behavior and beliefs are tied to emotion, and we must use the power of emotion to jump-start change.

## Selecting Questions for Discussion

- Why is it vital that principals develop core beliefs? What influenced you in adopting your own core beliefs?

- Discuss your reaction to Whitaker's central core belief that making it cool to care throughout the school is of paramount importance. Is this a valid core belief for other principals? Explain.

- Why does Whitaker downplay the importance of getting your faculty to go along with a particular initiative? What is a more significant goal?

- How can we ensure that our very best teachers are the ones placed on a pedestal by students, parents, and peers as our legendary teachers?

- Why is it important to consider the emotional side of teachers when implementing change? Discuss ways to deal with teachers resistant to change.

## Eliciting Journal Responses

Whitaker shares his own core beliefs in this chapter, most notably that he wanted it to be "cool to care" at his school. On p. 91, he describes "The Great Teacher," whom he identifies as "Mrs. Heart," as an example of a staff member who cared about her students and her school, and who made it "cool to care" for students in her classroom. In your own words, what is Whitaker's philosophy of education? What was Mrs. Heart's philosophy of education? Is this a philosophy with which you agree? Take a moment to describe your own philosophy of education, highlighting simple core beliefs to which you adhere.

## Interacting With Others

### I can see clearly now...

In this chapter, Whitaker stresses that core beliefs are central to any school's success and he offers his own core belief, his goal of making it "cool to care" at his school. Distribute the following nine statements to each participant. Each of these statements could possibly stand as a core belief of a principal. Ask every participant to consider the statements, assigning a 1, 2, or 3 to each, with 1 representing something that they would fervently support as a core belief; 2 indicating agreement with the statement, but not necessarily a core belief; and 3 representing something that they believe is not significant or with which they may even disagree. Next, arrange participants into groups of three or four to discuss their individual responses and to arrive at a group consensus. Post each statement on a piece of chart paper on the wall. Ask each group to record its rating of each statement (1, 2, or 3) on the chart paper. Engage the group at-large in a discussion of patterns of thought or areas of divergent thinking.

- In our school, we will do whatever it takes to teach, inspire, and motivate all learners, including both student and adult members.
- In our school, we will work collaboratively, focusing on results and learning, sharing strategies that engage learners, and seeking help in areas in which we are struggling to engage them.
- In our school, we will be visible throughout the school. Administrators will be regular and active in their visits to classrooms.
- In our school, there will be no pecking order among our staff members. Those who contribute to the overall group in advancing our vision will be valued and recognized, whether they have 1 or 31 years of experience.
- In our school, we will not give up on our students and will rely on each other in finding new ways to engage each and every student.
- In our school, we will not settle for good; instead, we will strive for greatness by continually exploring new ways of ensuring success for all learners.
- In our school, we will model lifelong learning. All teachers at our school will earn a master's degree. Many will also earn specialist's and doctoral degrees. Many teachers will become certified in the areas of reading, ESOL, and gifted instruction.

- In our school, we will display teacher and student work throughout the school and beyond. We will recognize and celebrate our successes.
- In our school, we will act on the premise that we are the variables at our school. Superior teaching and leadership are the primary determinants of student and school success. We will not blame outside forces for poor results; we will accept responsibility for all areas of our school's performance.

## Tell me what you see…

Have each participant read the passage below, which describes a school in Anywhere, USA. Then, working in groups of three to five, distribute ten pieces of cardstock paper, each large enough on which to write a sentence. Have group members discuss the scenario, and ask them to surmise, based on this description, the likely core beliefs, vision, and values that are in place and shared at the school. Each group should write at least ten possible statements that might apply based on the information included below. Place one piece of chart paper for each group on the walls of the room. Ask each group to tape its ten statements on a piece of chart paper and present the core beliefs of the school in Anywhere, USA as they discern them, explaining how they arrived at their answers and whether they agree with the beliefs in place at this school.

As you walk into the school located in Anywhere, USA, the first thing you notice is the amount of student work displayed on the walls of the school. There are also a number of framed photographs of teachers and students working and celebrating together adorning the walls. You step into the office and are greeted warmly by the receptionist, who welcomes you to Anywhere and asks if you would like a cup of coffee or a bottled water. She informs you that the administrators are not in the office at the moment, as they are visiting classrooms, but offers to find a student leader who can offer a tour of the school.

While touring the school with the student, you learn a great deal about the school. In the classrooms you visit, you see kids actively engaged in learning. Your student guide tells you that all students are required to complete all assignments. She says that failure is not an option at this school, and that if you do not turn work in on time, you will simply have to do it later, perhaps losing a privilege. As you pass one classroom, you notice a teacher other than the classroom teacher sitting in the back taking notes. Your student guide informs you that this is a teacher from another grade level who must be doing one of her peer observations. Although students seem to be producing quality work in each room, they also appear to be having fun—laughing, smiling, and interacting with each other and their teachers.

Outside several classrooms, you see adults working with small groups of students. Your guide informs you that these are parent volunteers. Your guide introduces you to Mr. Jones, an assistant principal you meet in the hallway. Mr. Jones greets you warmly and introduces several of the folks with him, who turn out to be teachers and administrators from another district who came to observe in the school for the day.

In several rooms you visit, teachers are obviously on planning time, but they are planning in small groups with their colleagues, examining student work, and sharing strategies with each other for increasing student engagement. In another classroom, a team of teachers is analyzing data from the previous year's standardized testing and establishing goals for the next nine weeks of instruction in terms of standards learned and anticipated performance on common assessments.

In nearly every classroom, you notice two things in common: the standard from the state curriculum being taught and learned is posted at the front of the room and one wall of the classroom is dedicated as the "Word Wall," with vocabulary from each academic discipline posted. As you enter the final classroom on your tour, you observe a lady talking to a class about setting and accomplishing goals. Your guide informs you that this is the principal of the school conducting a "guest" lesson.

On your return to the office, you meet a newspaper reporter and photographer who are there to do a feature on one of the teachers. The teacher was named Teacher of the Year for the entire system. Your student guide shakes your hand and thanks you for visiting their school. The receptionist offers you a colorful brochure describing the school, along with a copy of the most recent monthly newsletter.

## Notes

## Taking It Back

On p. 93 of the text, Whitaker states that in great schools, teachers tell stories about the teaching legends they have worked with. Write about one or more teachers at your current school whom you consider "legendary." Write about a teacher or principal in your own life who positively impacted you and whom you also consider a legend. Share these written stories with the teacher you are writing about by placing it in that teacher's mailbox. In the case of the teacher or principal who impacted you, consider mailing the writing to that teacher or principal or to one of their family members.

# Section Twelve

## *Chapter 15: Don't Need to Repair—Always Do Repair*

### Understanding Key Concepts

- Effective principals aim to treat people with respect ten days out of ten. They know that a relationship, once damaged, may never be the same.
- Effective principals are acutely sensitive to every thing they say and do.
- The best principals work to keep their relationships in good shape and teachers notice this. They also work hard to repair any relationships that become damaged.
- Great principals have a high knowledge of the staff beyond school. They inquire about families, personal lives, and outside interests.
- Principals must work with teachers in helping to build their "people skills." They focus on changing behaviors, without necessarily altering beliefs.
- One way we can repair relationships—and teach our teachers to repair damaged relationships—is by using the simple statement, "I am sorry that happened," with parents, students, or others who are upset. This is a powerful defuser.
- With all discipline matters, it is essential that we focus on prevention, not punishment. We cannot do anything about an incident that has occurred; we can work to prevent it from happening again.

## Selecting Questions for Discussion

- Discuss several ways that principals work to establish and maintain healthy professional relationships. Discuss techniques that principals must use in teaching students and teachers how to repair damaged relationships.

- Why is the simple phrase, "I am sorry that happened," such an effective first step in restoring a damaged relationship with a teacher, parent, or student?

- Why is it important for principals to become familiar with their teachers beyond the school setting?

- Whitaker states that the critical issue in working to change teacher behaviors is not *why* they change their behavior, but *whether* they change their behavior. Explain this statement.

- Why is it counterproductive to focus on getting a teacher to admit they were wrong? What is a more productive approach?

## Eliciting Journal Responses

Imagine (or draw on your own experience) a situation in which a parent is visibly upset with you about something that happened at school involving their son or daughter (e.g., a bad grade, a demeaning comment that was allegedly made by a teacher at your school about the child, a punishment with which they do not agree). Write about this situation and how it would play out if your immediate response was "I am sorry that happened." Write out a script of responses and follow-up replies in such a situation. Remember that you are not saying it was your fault or accepting blame; rather, you are simply starting off by expressing your sorrow that it happened.

## Interacting With Others

### Restoring and repairing…

The author advises educators to teach students to behave in a way that "restores" them in the eyes of the offended party. In a traditional approach to discipline, the focus may be on (a) What happened? (b) Who's to blame? and (c) What's the punishment? On the other hand, a restorative approach asks (a) What happened? (b) Who has been affected and how? (c) How can we put it right? and (d) What have we learned so that we can make different choices next time? Prior to class, create four scenarios that occur in school resulting in someone being adversely affected. Write these on index cards, and, after organizing the participants into four groups, distribute one card to each group. Situations might include a student consistently talks out in class; a student responds disrespectfully to a teacher; a student refuses to complete an assignment; and a student uses inappropriate or threatening language toward a classmate. Have each group analyze their assigned scenario and plan out a course of action based both on the traditional approach and the restorative approach. Have each group post its two plans on two different pieces of chart paper and present the plans to the group at-large. Discuss the benefits and disadvantages to the two approaches while focusing on the goals of restoration and repairing.

### All the things we say and do…

Effective principals are sensitive to everything they say and do. They must have excellent "people skills." Communication is not limited to only words; it also includes actions, including body language. Using this activity reinforces these understandings.

Prior to this activity, copy and cut apart each item on the list below. Provide one set of the 27 underlined items per group; each group must have three to five members. Provide each group a set of items and ask them to categorize the items into six groups based on similarities and differences. Do not give any other direction, other than to remind participants that the items all relate to some way in which we communicate—verbally or nonverbally—with others. Approximately 10–15 minutes should be enough time to group the items. Have groups share their categories and the discussions which ensued within their groups.

When participants are happy / resigned to the categories they have created and to which they have arranged items, the facilitator should reveal the actual category headings (Eye Contact; Facial Expressions; Gestures; Posture; Body

Orientation, and Proximity, Para Linguistics; and Humor). These are not distinguished to encourage group members to decide on category headings.

- Eye Contact
  - Signals interest in others
  - Increases the speaker's credibility
  - Conveys interest, concern, warmth
  - Helps regulate the flow of communication
- Facial Expressions
  - Powerful cues
  - Often contagious
  - Warm and approachable
  - People will react favorably
  - Perceived as warm and approachable
- Gestures
  - Failure to do so is perceived as boring and stiff
  - Lively and animated captures attention
  - Perceived as more interesting
  - Head nods indicate listening
- Posture, Body Orientation, and Proximity
  - Stand erect and lean slightly forward
  - Face each other
  - Cultural norms dictate a comfortable distance
  - Enables you to make better eye contact
  - Increases the opportunities for conversation
- Para Linguistics
  - Tone
  - Rhythm
  - Loudness
  - Inflection
  - Speaking in a monotone
- Humor
  - Often overlooked as a teaching tool
  - Releases stress and tension
  - Fosters a friendly environment
  - Must be appropriate

## Taking It Back

Take some time in the next few days at your school to focus on communicating with students, parents, and teachers. Ask several students who have attended your school for more than one year to meet with you in your office. Ask them to share something positive about a teacher they have had as well as things they may wish to see improved in the school, in and out of the classroom. Call five parents at random, asking them what they most appreciate about your school and what they would like to see changed. Ask three trusted teachers how they deal with difficult parents and tense situations with students. Make mental and written notes on the responses of all three stakeholder groups. At the next session, offer to share what you have learned about your school focusing on the areas of communication and relationships. Throughout this activity, keep in mind the important issues of sensitivity and confidentiality.

# Section Thirteen

## *Chapter 16: Set Expectations at the Start of the Year*
## *Chapter 17: Clarifying Your Core*

### Understanding Key Concepts

- One of the most exciting aspects of being a principal is that each day is so different. One of the most challenging aspects of being a principal is that each day is so different!
- The excitement of a new school year provides principals the opportunity to reestablish expectations, introduce changes, and move our faculty forward.
- Principals must help teachers establish classroom expectations for students. The key is to set expectations with great clarity and then establish relationships such that students want to meet these expectations.
- In terms of student misbehavior, effective teachers focus on prevention; ineffective teachers focus on revenge.
- As principals, we have a responsibility to support our teachers. This is essential. However, unless we shift a teacher's mindset away from revenge, that teacher will never feel supported. We must seek different solutions: students who do not repeat their misbehavior.
- Effective principals express clear expectations at the very first faculty meeting of the year. This sets in place an important benchmark that we can revisit if people go astray later in the year.
- Great principals emphasize and establish expectations that express their nonnegotiable core beliefs.
- It is unfair to expect people to adhere to your expectations if you do not establish them upfront. What's more, if you have not clearly identified expectations at the start of the year, they may be perceived as your expectations, not the school's expectations.
- The specifics of our expectations can vary from school to school. What is essential is that they are clearly established, focus on the future, and are consistently reinforced.
- Our teachers and people throughout our community talk about us as the principal. We can decide what we want those conversations to be like.
- Although principals work in a community of colleagues, at times we have to make decisions on our own. Without a core of firmly held beliefs, it is difficult to steer a steady course.
- Every principal has an impact on others. Great principals make a difference.

## Selecting Questions for Discussion

- Why is it so important that both principals and teachers set clear expectations at the beginning of each school year? How does relationship building impact the extent to which others adhere to our expectations?

- Describe the difference between effective and ineffective teachers in terms of classroom management. How can principals make both groups of teachers feel supported in the important area of student behavior?

- Once we establish clear expectations at the start of the school year, what are some ways that we can reinforce these throughout the school year?

- According to Whitaker, we should host a back-to-school night before the first day of school. Explain his rationale and whether you agree.

- According to Whitaker, we can decide what kinds of discussions others within the community are having about us in our role as principal. Explain how we control this.

- Discuss the difference between having an impact as a principal and making a difference as a principal.

## Eliciting Journal Responses

Take a moment to consider what is vitally important to you as a principal in terms of setting expectations for teachers at the outset of each school year. Whitaker shares three of his own expectations for teachers: (a) never use sarcasm, (b) never argue, and (c) never yell. Take a moment to decide on three expectations of your own. Brainstorm in writing how you can communicate your expectations clearly, ensure that your expectations are consistently reinforced, and how you will react when teachers fail to meet them.

## Interacting With Others

### 15 Things...

Type each of the "Fifteen Things That Matter Most" on a separate slip of paper. Tape each item on a separate desk around the room. Arrange participants into 15 groups (or have them work individually if there are 15 or fewer participants). Start each group at one of the 15 "stations" and have them spend 3 minutes reflecting on the item at that desk. Have them write examples from the book, or their own experience, which relate to the statement. Have them write why they feel the statement is important. After 5 minutes, call out for each group to rotate 1 desk (moving in numerical order, with those people at desk #15 rotating to desk #1). Repeat the process of reflecting on each statement until each participant/group has moved through all 15 stations. After reviewing the author's core beliefs, ask individuals to think about additional core beliefs not mentioned in the text that they personally feel are essential components of their personal mission as a teacher. Allow time for each participant to write two to four additional core beliefs they value as educators. Have each individual pair up with a classmate and share each other's core belief additions. Encourage individuals to share these with the whole group.

### What to say—on the very first day...

Have all principals consider the following: The first announcement of the first day of school may be the only day of the year in which you have almost everyone's (including teachers and students) rapt attention. You have read and discussed the 15 things that matter most as presented by the author. You have thought through expectations for your own school. Now is the time to present these expectations to your students (and teachers) for the first time for the new school year. Take the time now to write out exactly what you will say over the loudspeaker or on camera on that first day of school. Make it interesting, memorable, and concise. Is there a way that you could make your expectations known each and every day? Can you develop a catchy acronym or saying that can be incorporated into posters and other print materials to be distributed throughout the year? How will you make it a part of the everyday culture of your school?

Have all participants read their "first-day-of-school" announcement to the entire group. Group members should offer positive feedback as well as constructive criticism.

## Taking It Back

On p. 108 of the text, Whitaker suggests several ways to revisit expectations with teachers throughout the school year, including the idea of incorporating these expectations into a *Friday Focus* memo. Read the following example, written by Jeff Zoul and sent out to his staff on the first Friday of a school year. Think again about your own expectations for teachers and consider writing a similar memo. Save this to send out on the first Friday of the new school year.

### Friday Focus!

**"Schools are not buildings, curriculums, and machines. Schools are relationships and interactions among people" (Johnson & Johnson, 1989).***

I hope everyone enjoyed a productive and enjoyable week of preplanning activities. Although Monday will be my 24th "Opening Day," I never lose the nervous edge I felt on my very first day of school when I began my career as a first grade teacher in Gwinnett County. As we begin a new school year Monday, I hope you share my sense of excitement, rejuvenation, and anticipation of what will be a tremendous year of growth for our students and our staff.

As I will suggest on countless occasions during the course of this year, our success as professional educators will depend to some extent on our specific skills and the breadth of our knowledge base. However, I firmly believe that our character and our human relations skills are even more vital to our ultimate success with our students and our entire school community. Nearly every effective educator I have worked with in my career has excelled in the area of interpersonal skills. Although no list of such traits can be thoroughly exhaustive, I do hope that you will peruse those offered below. Let's focus on these human relations skills as we embark upon a noble journey: teaching young people who need and crave our guidance!

- Be willing to admit when you're wrong.
- Be able to laugh (have a good sense of humor) and cry (display empathy and sensitivity).
- Take time to help others.

*Johnson, D.W., & Johnson, R.T. (1989). *Leading the cooperative school* (p. 1). Edina, MN: Interaction Book Co.

- Remember how it felt to be a child.
- Be able to resolve conflicts between people.
- Enjoy working with people of all ages.
- Truly care about others.
- Realize that you can't please everyone.
- Be optimistic about people's motives.

Thank you all for your prodigious efforts this week; thank you all for the human relations skills you already possess and practice daily. Let's remember the importance of those listed above as we progress through this year. Remember to set expectations in your own classrooms and then go about building relationships such that your students will want to meet them. I can't wait to see you all in action next week! You hold the keys to success for our students; unlock their hearts and their minds. Have an outstanding week and knock 'em dead (not literally, of course)!

Happy Weekend———Jeff

---

# Fifteen Things That Matter Most

1. Great principals remember that it is people, not programs, that determine the quality of the school.
2. Great principals know that they are the variable responsible for all aspects of the school.
3. Great principals treat everyone with respect, ten days out of ten.
4. Great principals consistently filter out negatives that do not matter and, instead, focus on the positive.
5. Great principals know that they cannot expect teachers to improve if they do not teach them new strategies.
6. Great principals know the two best ways to improve a school: by improving teachers who are already in place or by hiring better teachers to replace them.
7. Great principals keep standardized testing in perspective. They understand its importance, but focus on what is truly important—student learning.
8. Great principals understand that it is not always possible to change beliefs, but that it is possible to change behaviors.
9. Great principals want teachers to be loyal to the students. Great principals are loyal to teachers, to students, and to the school.
10. Before making any important decision, great principals ask themselves one central question: *What will my best teachers think?*
11. Great principals continually ask themselves who is most comfortable and who is least comfortable with each decision they make. They treat everyone as if they are good.
12. Great principals value high-achieving teachers, making sure to provide them with autonomy and recognition.
13. Great principals communicate core beliefs and establish a school climate in which it is cool to care.
14. Great principals work hard to keep their relationships in good repair—to avoid personal hurt and to repair any possible damage.
15. Great principals establish clear expectations at the beginning of the school year and follow them consistently throughout the year.

If you would like information about inviting Todd Whitaker to speak to your group, please contact him at t-whitaker@indstate.edu or at his web site www.toddwhitaker.com or (812) 237-2904.

Order form on page 90

Order form on page 90

# Seven Simple Secrets:

## What the BEST Teachers Know and Do

### Annette Breaux & Todd Whitaker

"Easy to read and with great use of humor, this is a wonderful book for new teachers and their mentors."

*Sharon Weber, Principal*
*Bell Township Elementary School, PA*

Implementing these secrets will change your life both in and out of the classroom. But most importantly, they will enhance the lives of every student you teach!

This book reveals—

- The Secret of Planning
- The Secret of Classroom Management
- Secret of Instruction
- The Secret of Attitude
- The Secret of Professionalism
- The Secret of Effective Discipline
- The Secret of Motivation and Inspiration

*2006. 150 pp. (est.) Paperback. 1-59667-021-5. $29.95 plus shipping and handling.*

Order form on page 90

## Dealing with Difficult Parents (And with Parents in Difficult Situations)

**Todd Whitaker & Douglas J. Fiore**

"This book is an easy read with common sense appeal. The authors are not afraid to share their own vulnerability and often demonstrate a sense of humor."

*Gale Hulme, Program Director, Georgia's Leadership Institute for School Improvement*

This book helps teachers, principals, and other educators develop skills in working with the most difficult parents in the most challenging situations.

It shows you how to avoid the "trigger" words that serve only to make bad situations worse and how use the right words and phrases to help you develop more positive relationships with parents.

*2001. 175 pp. Paperback. 1-930556-09-8. $29.95 plus shipping and handling.*

## Improving Your School One Week at a Time:

### Building the Foundation for Professional Teaching and Learning

**Jeffrey Zoul**

This book displays 37 "Friday Focus" memos, also downloadable from Eye On Education's web site. Each memo provides insight into a specific aspect of teaching and learning for all to reflect on throughout the year. The memos offer inspiration about themes including School Climate and Culture, Effective Teaching, Professional Development, and more.

*2007. 190 pp. Paper. 1-59667-7027-4. $29.95 plus shipping and handling.*

Order form on page 90

# Teaching Matters

## Motivating & Inspiring Yourself

### Todd and Beth Whitaker

"This book makes you want to be the best teacher you can be."

*Nancy Fahnstock,*
*Godby High School*
*Tallahassee, FL*

Celebrate the teaching life! This book helps teachers

- rekindle the excitement of the first day of school all year long
- approach every day in a "Thank God it is Monday" frame of mind
- not let negative people ruin your day
- fall in love with teaching all over again

*2002. 150 pp. Paperback. 1-930556-35-7. $24.95 plus shipping and handling.*

# Six Types of Teachers

## Recruiting, Retaining, and Mentoring the Best

### Douglas J. Fiore and Todd Whitaker

This book sharpens your ability to hire new teachers, improve the ones already there, and keep your best and brightest on board.

*2005. 176 pp. Paperback. 1-930556-85-3. $29.95 plus shipping and handling.*

Order form on page 90

# Dealing with Difficult Teachers

## Second Edition

### Todd Whitaker

Whether you are a teacher, administrator, or fill some other role in your school, difficult teachers can make your life miserable. This book shows you how to handle staff members who

- ♦ gossip in the teacher's lounge.
- ♦ consistently say "it won't work" when any new idea is suggested.
- ♦ undermine your efforts toward school improvement.
- ♦ negatively influence other staff members.

*2002. 208 pp. Paperback. 1-930556-45-4. $29.95 plus shipping and handling.*

# Feeling Great!

## The Educator's Guide for Eating Better, Exercising Smarter, and Feeling Your Best

### Todd Whitaker and Jason Winkle

Educator's spend so much time taking care of others that we sometimes forget to take care of ourselves! This book will help teachers, principals, professors, and all educators find time in our busy schedules to focus on our physical self.

*2002. 150 pp. Paperback. 1-930556-38-1. $24.95 plus shipping and handling.*

Order form on page 90

Order form on page 90

# ORDER FORM

Qty.

____ SEVEN SIMPLE SECRETS: What the BEST Teachers Know and Do! Breaux and Whitaker. $29.95 plus shipping and handling.

____ WHAT GREAT PRINCIPALS DO *DIFFERENTLY:* 15 Things That Matter Most. Whitaker. $29.95 plus shipping and handling.

____ TEACHING MATTERS: Motivating and Inspiring Yourself. Whitaker and Whitaker. $24.95 plus shipping and handling.

____ DEALING WITH DIFFICULT TEACHERS, Second Edition. Whitaker. $29.95 plus shipping and handling.

____ MOTIVATING AND INSPIRING TEACHERS: The Educational Leader's Guide for Building Staff Morale. Whitaker, Whitaker, and Lumpa. $34.95 plus shipping and handling.

____ SIX TYPES OF TEACHERS: Recruiting, Retaining, and Mentoring the Best. Fiore and Whitaker. $29.95 plus shipping and handling.

____ DEALING WITH DIFFICULT PARENTS (AND WITH PARENTS IN DIFFICULT SITUATIONS). Whitaker and Fiore. $29.95 plus shipping and handling.

____ GREAT QUOTES FOR GREAT EDUCATORS. Whitaker and Lumpa. $29.95 plus shipping and handling.

____ FEELING GREAT! The Educator's Guide for Eating Better, Exercising Smarter, and Feeling Your Best. Whitaker and Winkle. $24.95 plus shipping and handling.

____ WHAT GREAT TEACHERS DO *DIFFERENTLY:* 14 Things That Matter Most. Whitaker. $29.95 plus shipping and handling.

____ STUDY GUIDE: What Great Teachers Do *Differently*. Whitaker and Whitaker. $16.95 plus shipping and handling.

____ IMPROVING YOUR SCHOOL ONE WEEK AT A TIME: Building the Foundation for Professional Teaching and Learning. Zoul. $29.95 plus shipping and handling.

____ **Save $30!** Order all 12 books for $311.40 plus shipping and handling.

## HOW TO ORDER

Phone (888) 299-5350
Fax (914) 833-0761
E-mail *sales@eyeoneducation.com*
Web *www.eyeoneducation.com*
Or mail your order to:

EYE ON EDUCATION

**6 Depot Way West**
**Larchmont, NY 10538**

## Shipping and Handling

1 book - Add $6.00
2 books - Add $10.00
3 books - Add $13.00
4 books - Add $15.00
5–7 books - Add $17.00
8–11 books - Add $19.00
12–15 books - Add $25.00
More—Feel free to call

N.Y. and N.J. residents add sales tax.
Prices subject to change without notice.

**You can order *ONLINE* too!**
**www.eyeoneducation.com**

METHOD OF PAYMENT (choose one): ☐ Check (enclosed) ☐ Credit Card ☐ Purchase Order

Purchase Order # or Credit Card # with exp. date

Your e-mail address (for free excerpts from new and future titles)

**SHIPPING ADDRESS:** **SCHOOL?** ☐ **HOME?** ☐

Name

School

Street Address

City State Zip

Phone

**BILLING ADDRESS FOR PURCHASE ORDERS:**

Name

School

Street Address

City State Zip

Phone

Your Job Title— ☐ Principal ☐ Teacher ☐ District Administrator ☐ Other ____________ SGP